AF428225

A CLOSER LOOK AT SILICON

Chemistry Book for Elementary | Children's Chemistry Books

Speedy Publishing LLC

40 E. Main St. #1156

Newark, DE 19711

www.speedypublishing.com

Copyright 2017

Silicon is classified as a metalloid and is the eighth most abundant element of our universe and the second most abundant in Earth's crust, following oxygen. It has many uses including, but not limited to, making greases, lubricants, rubber materials, caulks and waterproofing materials. In its pure form, silicon is used with the manufacturing of semiconductor chips for electronics.

Read further to learn more about its characteristics, how it was discovered and more.

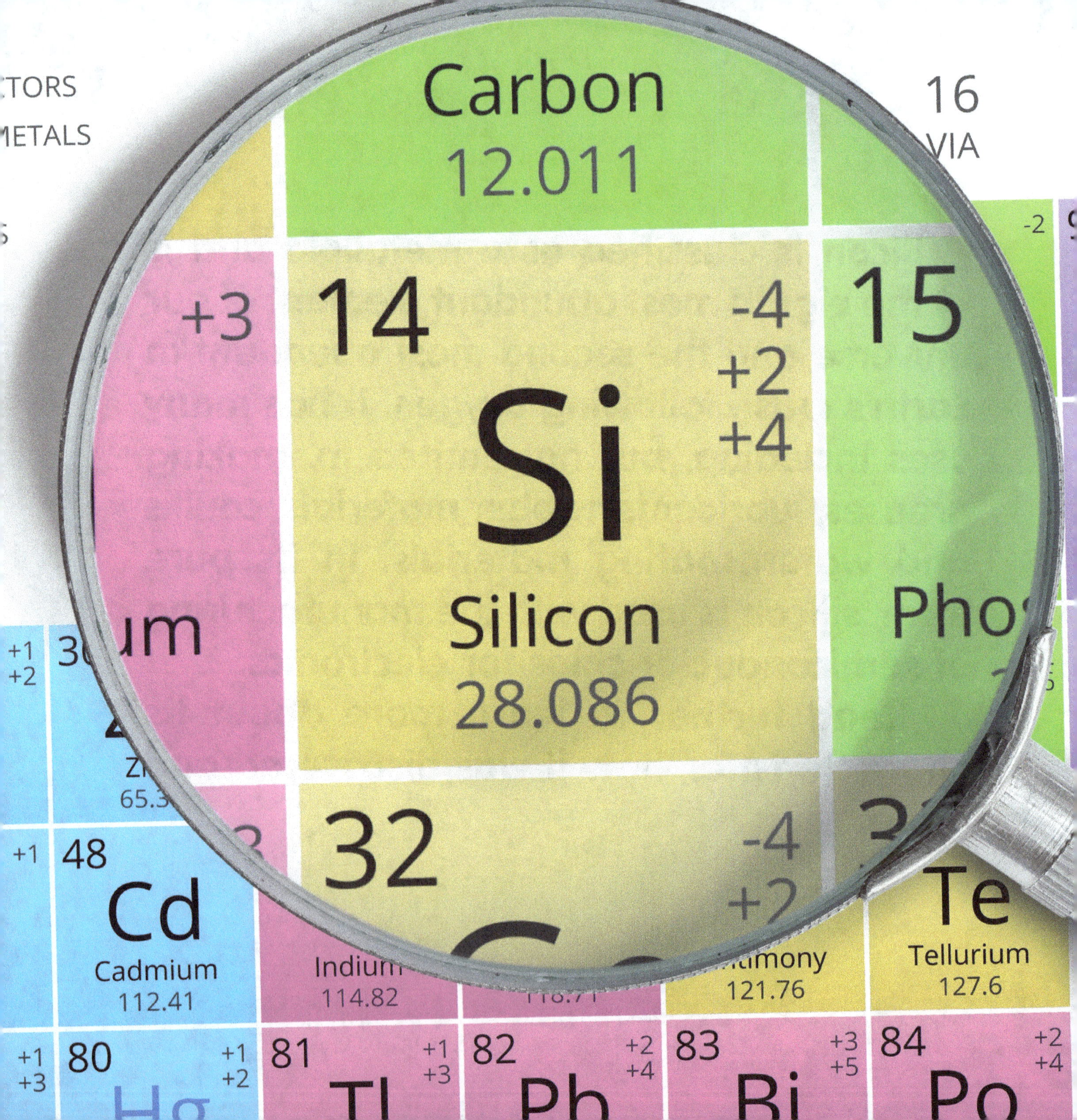
CTORS
METALS
Carbon
12.011
16
VIA
+3
14
-4
+2
+4
15
Si
Silicon
28.086
Phos
um
32
-4
+2
+1
+2
65.3
+1
48
Cd
Cadmium
112.41
Indium
114.82
Antimony
121.76
Te
Tellurium
127.6
+1
+3
80
Hg
+1
+2
81
Tl
+1
+3
82
Pb
+2
+4
83
Bi
+3
+5
84
Po
+2
+4

CHARACTERISTICS AND PROPERTIES OF SILICON

Its symbol is Si and it has an atomic number of 14 and atomic weight of 28.085. At room temperature, it is a solid. It is the second element in column 14 of the periodic table. Its atoms contain 14 protons and 14 electrons and has 4 valence electrons in its outer shell.

Silicon is a solid under standard conditions. In its random (amorphous) form it appears to be a brown powder. When in a crystalline form, it appears as a silver-gray metallic looking material which is strong and brittle.

It is known to be a semiconductor, which means it has electronic conductivity between a conductor and

insulator. With temperature, this conductivity increases. This makes is a
valuable element for electronics.

silicon crystal

Since it contains four valence electrons, it can create ionic or covalent bonds, either sharing or donating is four shell electrons. Accordingly, it is relatively inert and will not react with water or oxygen when in its solid form.

Silicon is unique in that it can expand like water when frozen.

WHERE CAN IT BE FOUND ON EARTH?

The Earth's crust is made up of approximately 28% of silicon. Typically, it is not found in its free form on earth, but can usually be found in silicate minerals. The Earth's crust consists of about 90% of these minerals. Silica, also known as silicon dioxide (SiO2) is one of the more common compounds.

Silica sand

Asbestos

Silica has the ability to take on various forms, such as quartz, flint and sand. Other silicon rocks and minerals include asbestos, clay, mica, diorite, talc and granite. It can also be found in gems such as amethysts, agates and opals.

HOW DO WE USE IT TODAY?

Silicon is useful in a variety of materials and applications. Most of the applications using silicon are silicate minerals, including glass (which is made from sand), abrasives and ceramics (which are made from clay). Silicates are also useful in making Portland cement which is used in making stucco and concrete.

Silicon sealant

Silicon can also be used in making synthetic compounds known as silicones. These silicones are useful in making caulks, waterproofing materials, rubber materials, greases and lubricants. In its pure form it is used for manufacturing semiconductor chips used in electronics. These chips create the brains for today's electronics, including mobile phones, video game consoles, televisions and computers.

It is also utilized in metal alloys along with steel, iron and aluminum.

HOW WAS SILICON DISCOVERED?

In 1789, Antoine Lavoisier, a French chemist, was among the first scientists to realize there might be an additional element in the substance quartz. Scientists continued to research quartz, but Jons Jakob Berzelius, a Swedish chemist, was the first to isolate the element of Silicon and produced the first sample in 1824.

Antoine Lavoisier

Jöns Jakob Berzelius

WHERE DID ITS NAME COME FROM?

The name is a derivative of the Latin term "silicus" which means "flint". As mentioned earlier, the mineral flint consists of silicon.

ISOTOPES

Silicon takes place organically in one of these stable three isotopes: silicon-28, silicon-29, and silicon-30. Approximately 92% of silicon is known as silicon-28.

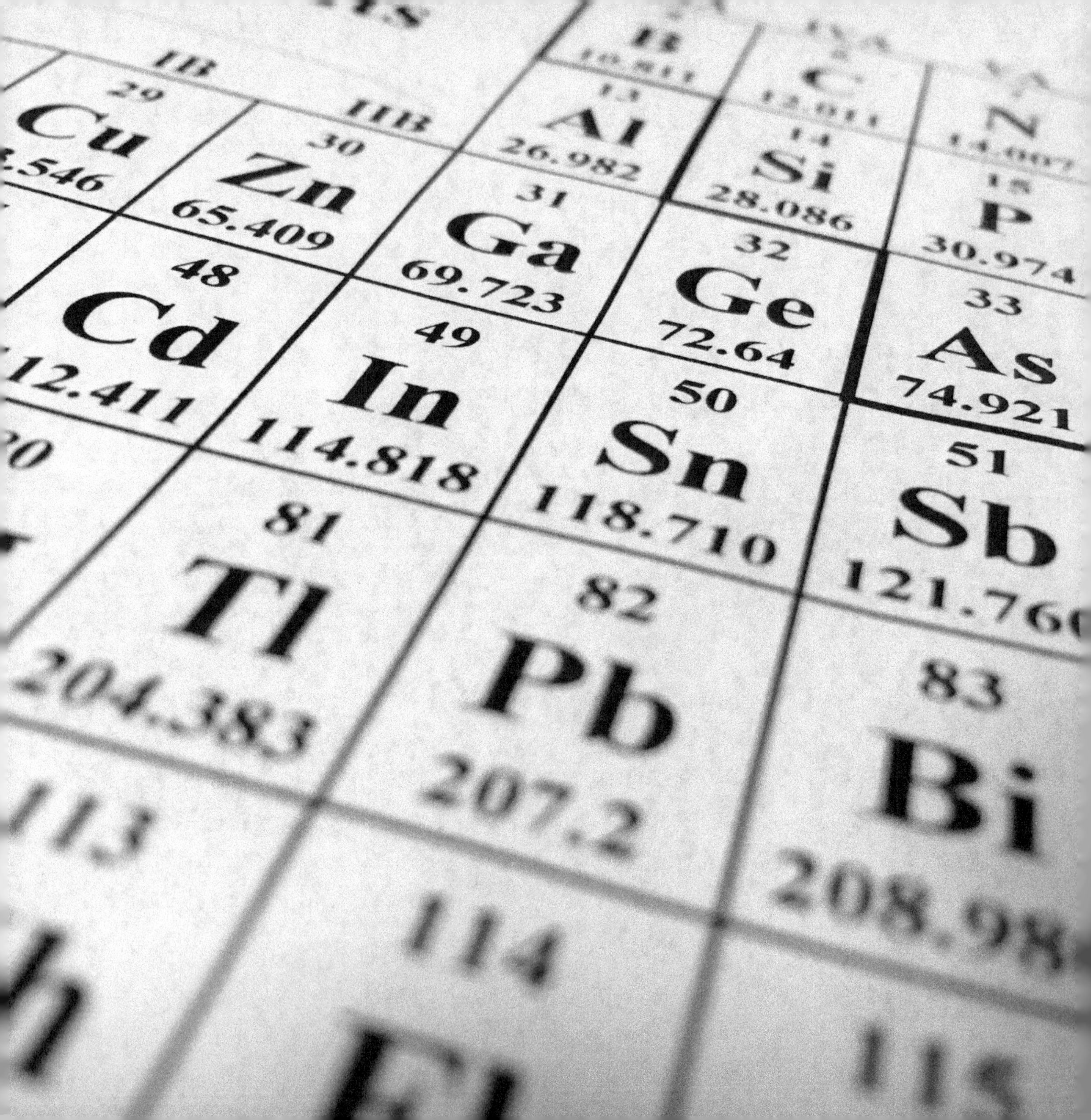

IB	IIB	IIIA	IVA	VA
29 Cu 63.546	**30** Zn 65.409	**13** Al 26.982	**14** Si 28.086	**7** N 14.007
48 Cd 112.411	**31** Ga 69.723	**32** Ge 72.64	**6** C 12.011	**15** P 30.974
	49 In 114.818	**50** Sn 118.710	**33** As 74.921	
81 Tl 204.383		**82** Pb 207.2	**51** Sb 121.760	
		114	**83** Bi 208.98	

METALLOIDS

The periodic table contains a group of elements known as Metalloids. They can be found left of the non-metals and right of the post-transition metals. They have similar properties with metals and non-metals.

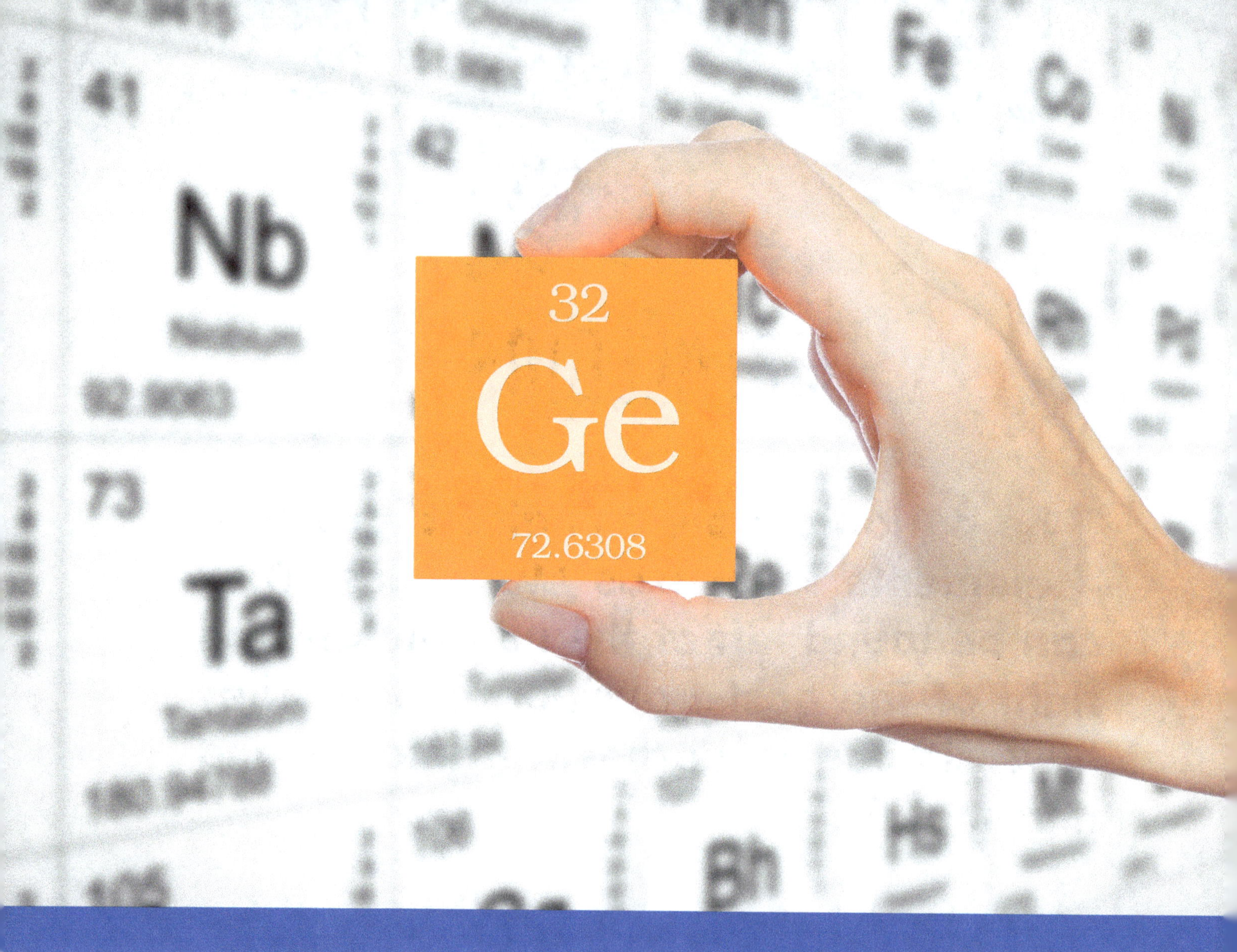

Those elements typically considered to be metalloids include tellurium, anti-mony, arsenic, germanium, silicon and

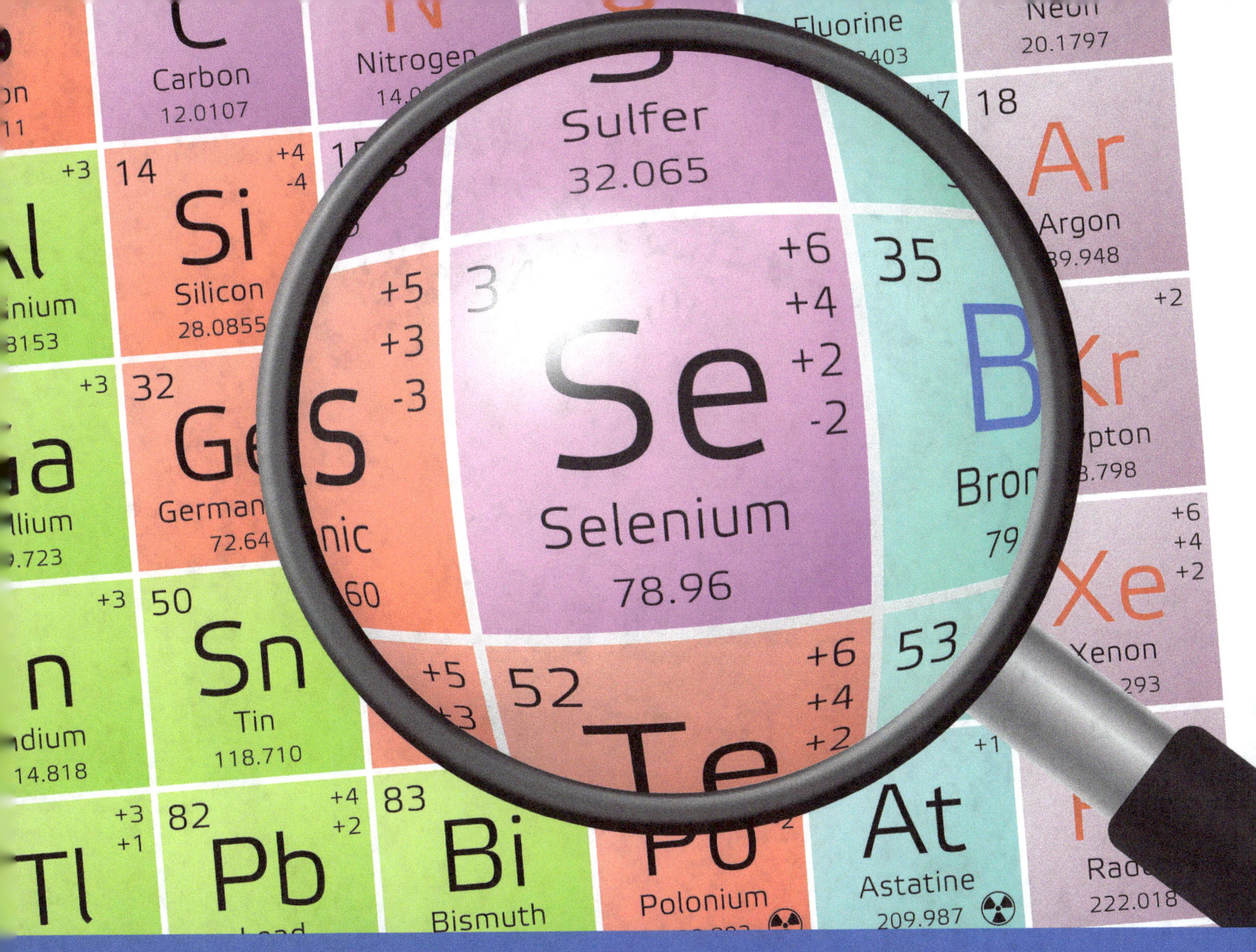

boron. Selenium and polonium are occasionally included in this list as well.

ETALS
IIIA
IVA
5 +3
B
Boron
10.81
6
Silicon
28.086
12
IIB
13
+3
32 -4
+2
+4
Ge
Germanium
72.64
33
+1
+2
30
Zn
Zinc
65.39
+1
48
Cd
Cadmium
112.41
50
Sn
+1
+3
80
Hg
Mercury
200.59
+1
+2
81
Tl
Thallium
204.38
+3
+5
84
Bi
Bismuth
+1
112
+1
+3
113

They share quite a few similar properties, such as:

- They are brittle, but appear to be metal

- Typically, they have the ability to form alloys with metals.

- Silicon and germanium, to name a few, can become electrical conductors under certain circumstances, and are referred to as semiconductors.

- Under standard conditions, they are in a solid form.

- Mostly, they are nonmetallic in their chemical behavior.

Silicon is the most abundant metalloid on Earth. Following oxygen, it is the second most abundant of the elements in Earth's crust. Tellurium is the least abundant which is also one of the rarest of the stable elements on Earth, similar to platinum. The following list is of the metalloids in order of their abundance in the crust of the Earth: Silicon, Boron, Germanium, Arsenic, Antimony and Tellurium.

Boron

WHAT IS A METALLOID

Metalloids are known as an element group in the periodic table. They can be found at the left of the non-metals and at the right of the post-transition metals. They have some common properties with metals and some common properties with non-metals. Included in this group are tellurium, antimony, arsenic, germanium, silicon, and boron. There are a few elements that are sometimes included in this group with are polonium and selenium.

WHAT ARE ELEMENTS?

An element is a substance that is pure and created from a single type of atom. The element is the basic building block for matter. Gold, iron, hydrogen, oxygen, and helium are considered as elements.

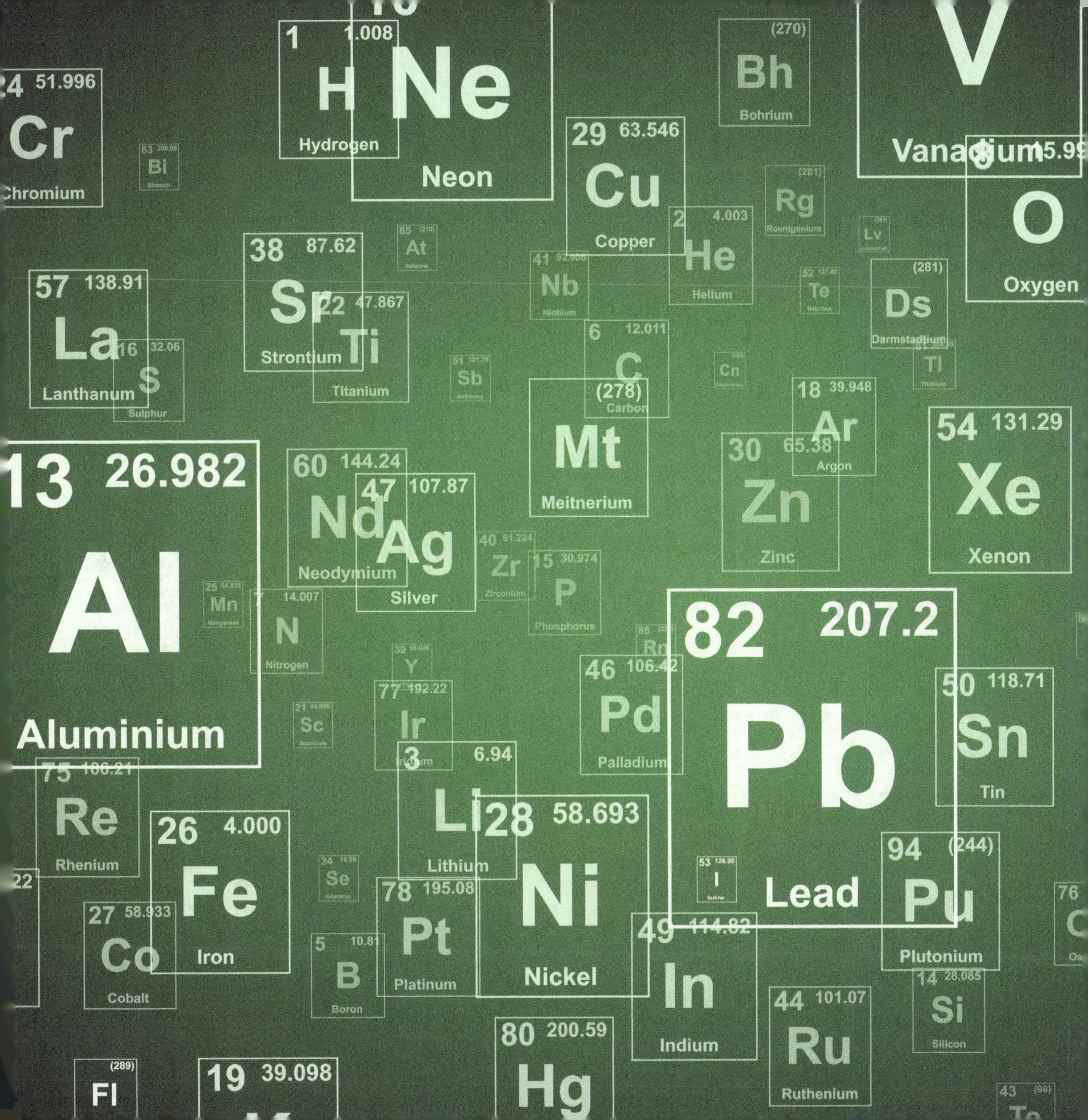

PERIODIC TABLE OF THE ELEMENTS

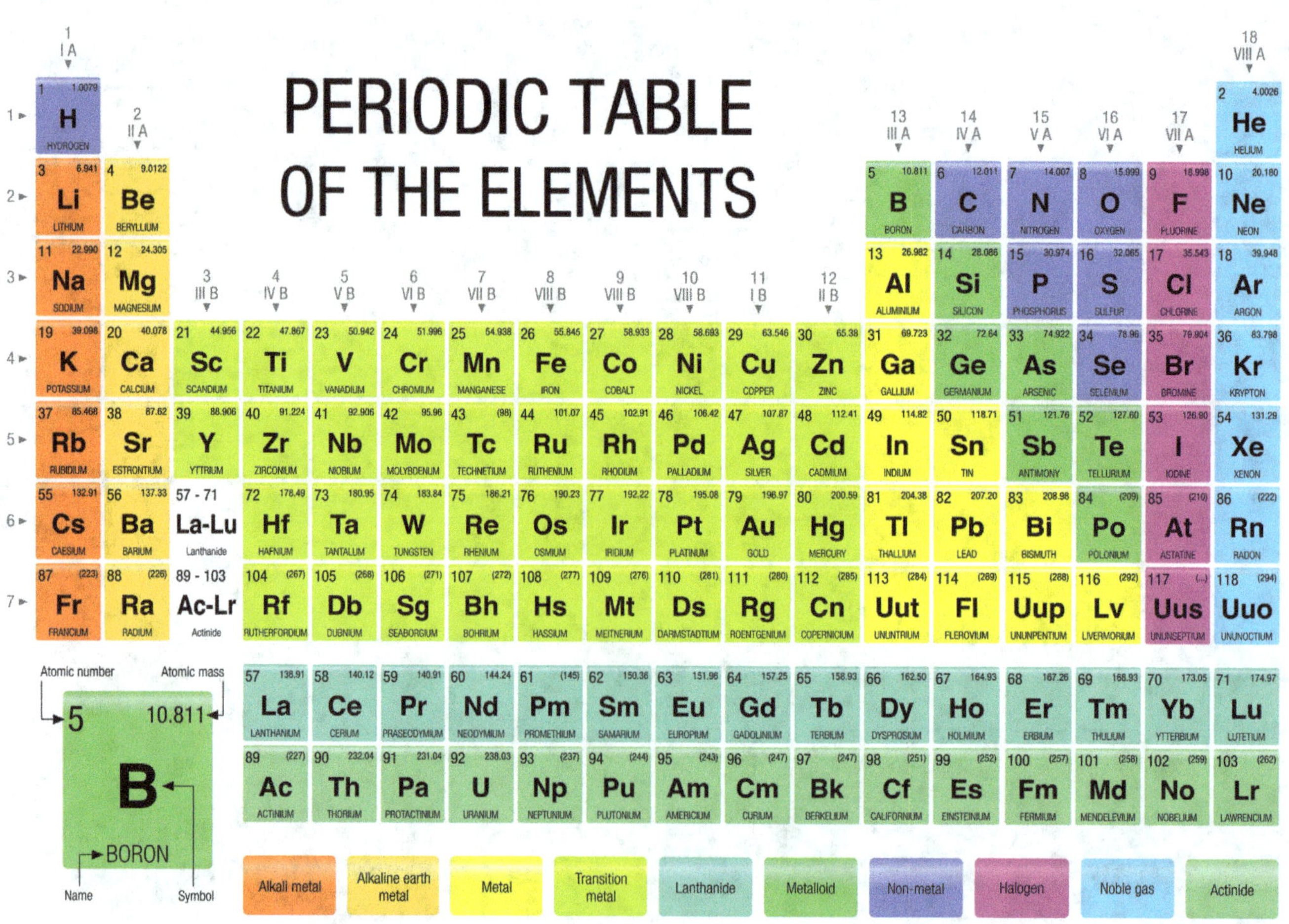

Of importance to the element is its atomic number. This number indicates how many protons are contained in the atom. No two atomic numbers are the same. Hydrogen contains 1 proton indicating an atomic number of 1. There are 79 protons in each atom of gold, making its atomic number 79.

There are currently 118 elements. There are only 94 believed to exist naturally on Earth.

Below is a list of elements that occasionally might be grouped with others if they have properties that are similar.

Noble Gases are radon, xenon, argon, neon, krypton, and helium. Their outer shell is filled with electrons. Consequently, they are not able to react with other elements. They are the elements used to produce the vibrant colors in lighted signs.

Periodic Table

Atomic nomber

Symbol

Name

Atomic Mass

noble gases

2	10	18	36	54	86	118
He	**Ne**	**Ar**	**Kr**	**Xe**	**Rn**	**Uuo**
Helium	Neon	Argon	Krypton	Xenon	Radon	Ununoctium
4.003	20.180	39.948	84.798	131.294	222.018	unknown

EPS 10

Periodic Table

Atomic
nomber

Symbol

Name

Atomic Mass

alkali metals

3	11	19	37	55	87
Li	**Na**	**K**	**Rb**	**Cs**	**Fr**
Lithium	Sodium	Potassium	Rubidium	Cesium	Francium
6.941	22.990	39.098	85.468	132.905	223.020

EPS 10

Alkali Metals include, but are not limited to, sodium, potassium, and lithium. They only have 1 electron in their outer shell which makes them reactive.

Actinides, lanthanides, alkali earth metals, transition metals, halogens, and nonmetals are examples of other groups of elements that might react with other elements.

WHAT ARE ISOTOPES?

Isotopes are atoms that contain a different number of neutrons but contain the exact same numbers of protons and electrons. The element remains the same even though the number of neutrons has changed. Atoms having a different number of neutrons are known as "isotopes" of that element.

Polycrystalline silicon

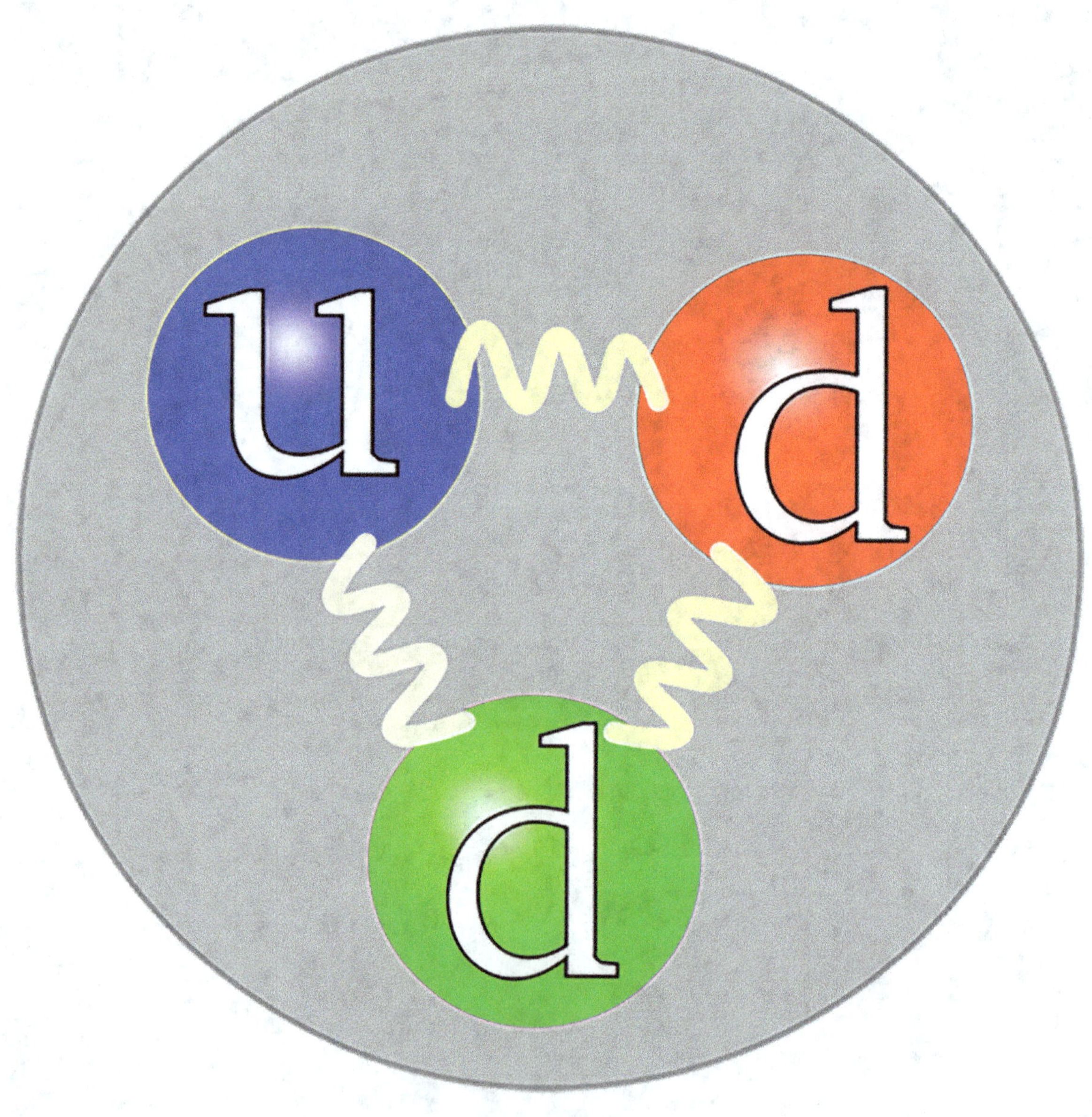

u
d
d
Neutron

Since a neutron doesn't have any electrical charge, changing its number of neutrons will not affect its chemistry, but will change its mass. We identify isotopes by their mass, which is the sum of its protons and neutrons.

Typically, we write Isotopes in two different ways. They both include its mass, which is found by using the formula mass = (number of protons) + (number of neutrons). The first method indicates the mass in superscript before the element's symbol. 4He is one example.

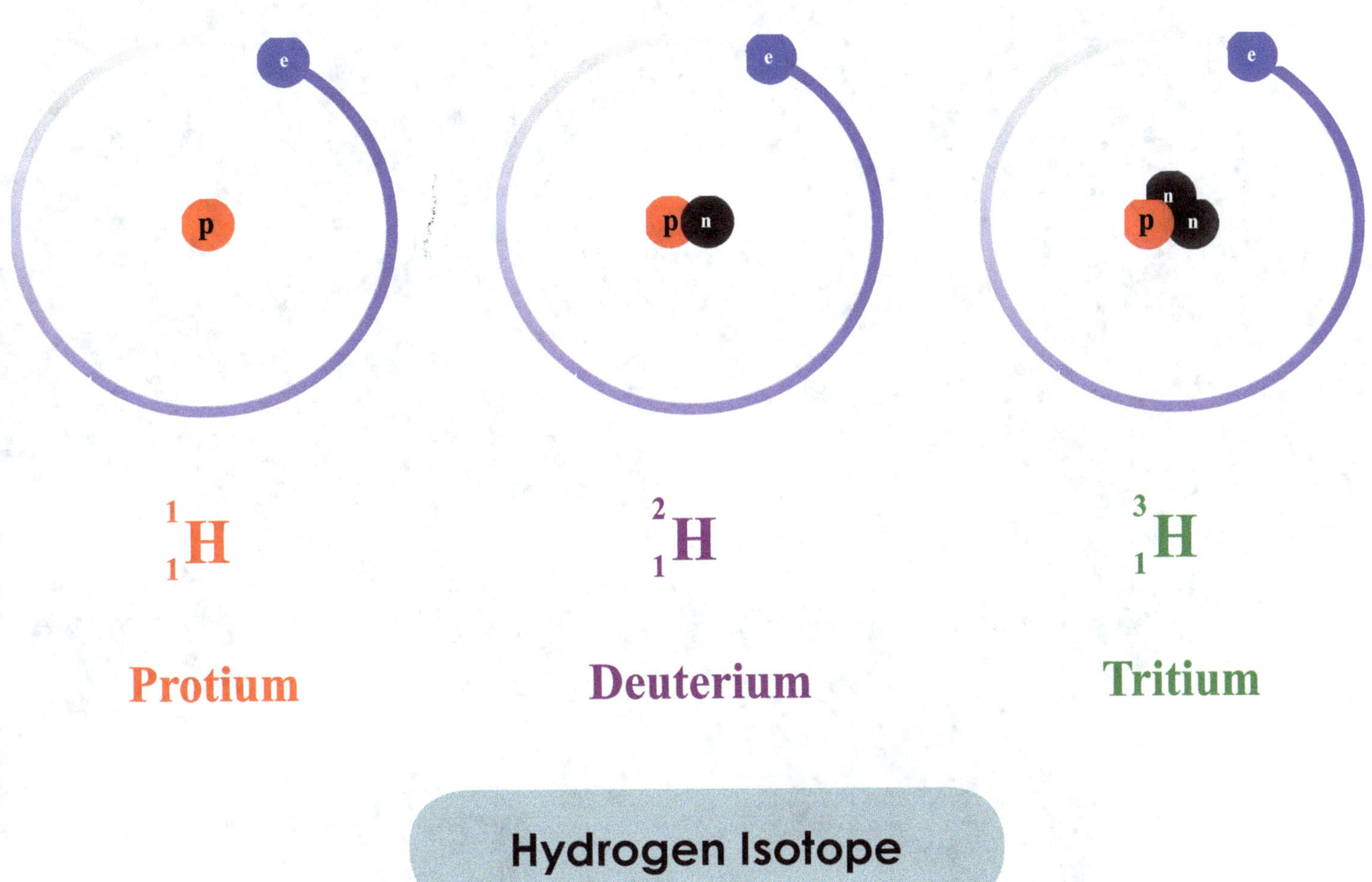

e
p
$^1_1$H
Protium
e
p n
$^2_1$H
Deuterium
e
n
p n
$^3_1$H
Tritium
Hydrogen Isotope

Silicon Optics

The second method is spelling it out, and placing its mass after the dash placed next to the name of the element. Helium-4 is an example, using the same element as we did in the previous paragraph.

An isotope might be stable or unstable. When unstable, an isotope decays with time, eventually turning into another isotope or element, and considered to be radioactive. Stables isotopes are elements mostly found in nature. The isotope considered to be the most stable is Tin, and it consists of ten varying stable isotopes.

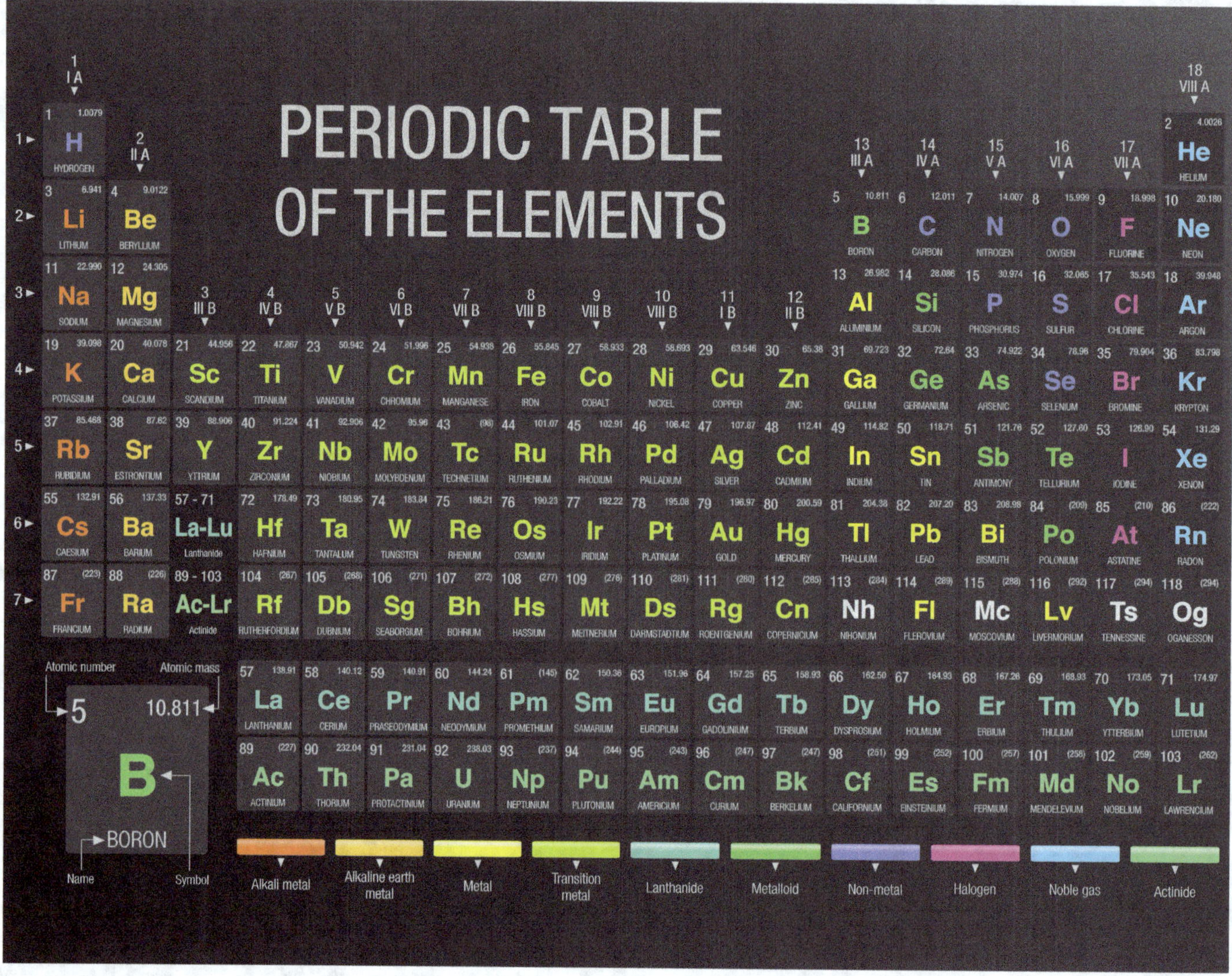

PERIODIC TABLE
OF THE ELEMENTS
Atomic number
Atomic mass
BORON
Name
Symbol
Alkali metal
Alkaline earth metal
Metal
Transition metal
Lanthanide
Metalloid
Non-metal
Halogen
Noble gas
Actinide

THE PERIODIC TABLE OF ELEMENTS

Elements are listed on the Periodic Table of Elements and are categorized by the structure of their atoms, which includes the number of protons and electrons that are in its outer shell. They are listed top to bottom and left to right by their atomic number.

The name "periodic" stems from the fact that the elements are aligned in periods of cycles. Some columns were skipped to enable elements that contain identical numbers of valence electrons are listed in the same column. The horizontal rows are referred to as a period.

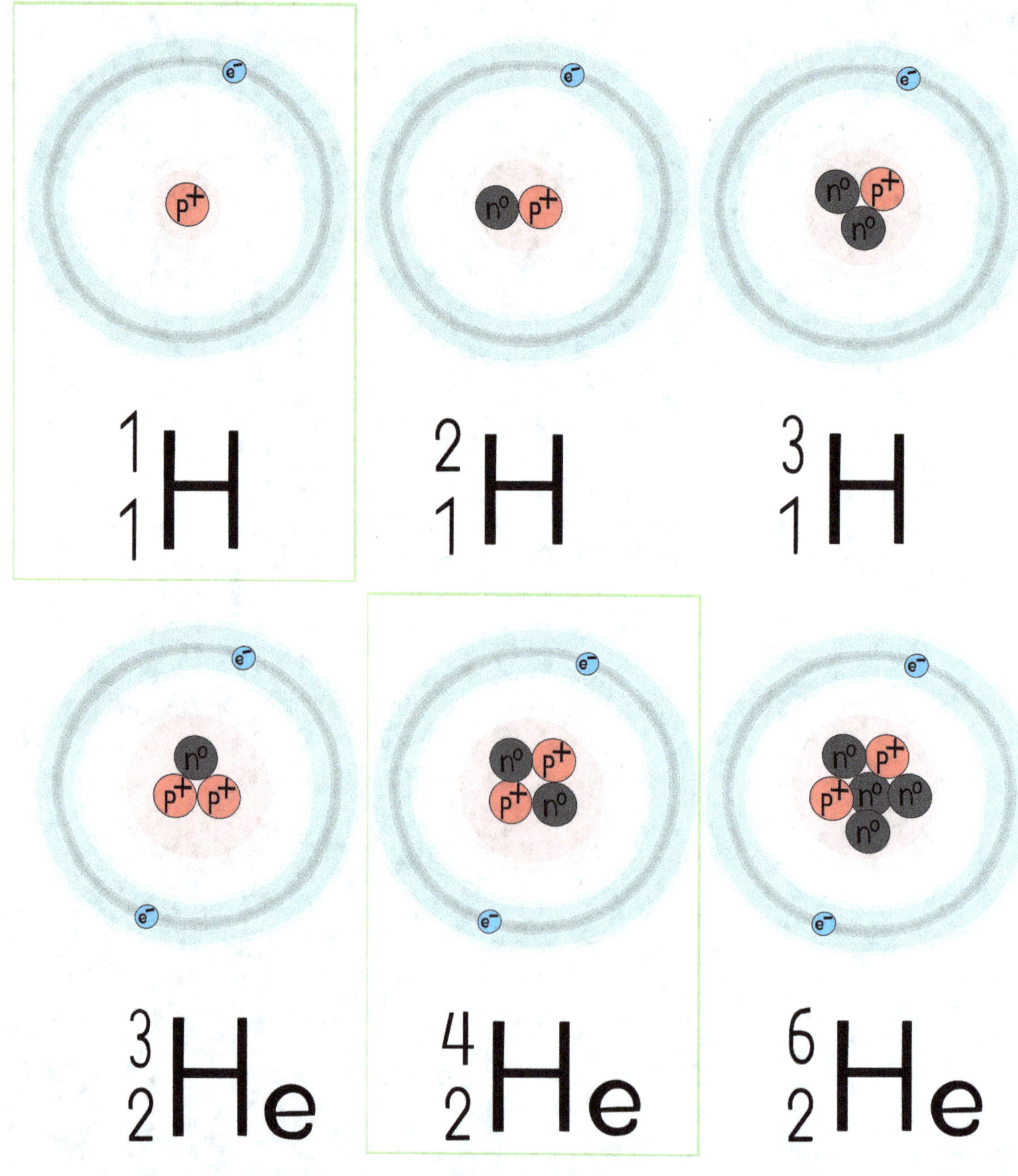

Isotopes of hydrogen and helium

They consist of seven, maybe eight total periods. The first period contains two elements, hydrogen and helium. The sixth period has 32 elements. Located at the left of each period are elements consisting of 1 electron in its outer shell, and the ones to the right have a full outer shell.

Now that you have learned about the element silicon, you can find answers to any questions you might have about this or any other elements found on the periodic table by going to your local library, researching the internet, or ask questions of your teachers, family, and friends.

Visit
BABY PROFESSOR
EDUCATION KIDS
www.BabyProfessorBooks.com
to download Free Baby Professor eBooks and view
our catalog of new and exciting Children's Books